Powershell

The What, Who and How of Powershell

David Chang

Legal & Disclaimer

The content and information in this book have been provided for educational and entertainment purposes only.

The content and information contained in this book have been compiled from sources deemed reliable, and it is accurate to the best of the Author's knowledge, information, and belief. However, the Author cannot guarantee its accuracy and validity and cannot be held liable for any errors and/or omissions. Further, changes are periodically made to this book as and when needed. Where appropriate and/or necessary, you must consult a professional (including but not limited to your doctor, attorney, financial advisor or such other professional advisor) before using any of the suggested remedies, techniques, or information in this book.

Upon using the contents and information contained in this book, you agree to hold harmless the Author from and against any damages, costs, and expenses, including any legal fees potentially resulting from the application of any of the information provided by this book. This disclaimer applies to any loss, damages or injury caused by the use and application, whether directly or indirectly, of any advice or information presented, whether for breach of contract, tort, negligence, personal injury, criminal intent, or under any other cause of action.

POWERSHELL

ISBN-10: 1548542725
ISBN-13: 978-1548542726

CONTENTS

INTRODUCTION

In today's highly competitive industry, achieving success and establishing a reputable name in the niche you have chosen takes enough amount of time and effort. Especially in today's modern era, technology plays an integral role in any business's success. This is why you need to adapt to these changes and trends.

Program software is one of the newest trends in the market, promising an efficient and productive result. Software programs served as applications that enable computers to solve any challenges while operating in an efficient manner. Their functions and designs may differ depending on the problem's nature they make to solve.

In the software program industry, Powershell is

known as one of the most reliable applications one should not overlook. This book aims to give readers knowledge of Powershell to confidently have an understanding of the basics of what this programming software can do as well as its potential both for project management and overall productivity.

WHAT IS POWERSHELL AND HOW IT WORKS WITH MICROSOFT

Powershell is a scripting language and automation platform for Windows and Windows Server. It empowers users to make their system management straightforward. What makes this programming software unique among other text-based shells is that, it connects the power of .NET framework, which offers rich objects and a large variety of integral functionality. This is important for taking over the Windows environment.

Above the standard command line shell, Windows Powershell Integrated Scripting Environment (ISE) can also be found. It is a graphical user edge that enables users to easily make various scripts without having the need to type each command within the command line. Powershell's first version was released in 2006 of November for Windows Vista, Windows Server 2003 and Windows XP.

Powershell Desired State Configuration (DSC) is also accessible in this programming software. It is a platform for checking and ensuring the system's declarative state. Desired State Configurations will allow users to scale intricate operations across environments, spot on configuration drift and empower management collaboration. The newest version of Powershell is Windows Powershell 5.0, which is being delivered through default using Windows 10. Also, it works with Windows 7 Service Pack 1, Windows 8.1, Windows Server 2012, Windows Server 2012 R2 and Windows Server 2008 R2.

Why Powershell?

You may often keep on asking what is so great about this software program, and why do you need to try it for your business.

Well, let me give you several reasons as to why Powershell is worth every single penny of your investment.

In addition to being a scripting language and a command line shell, it is also...

- **Object-based** – giving you an outstanding flexibility. You can be able to take actions such as sort, filter, compare, group, measure, etc. as they move across the pipeline. Users can also work with methods and properties, instead of raw text. Such a great convenience! I know how frustrating it is decoding and programmatically using text based output, which is why Powershell can be your best friend regarding this matter.

- **Compatible with various technologies including COM, ADSI, WMI, Cisco UCS, XenDesktop, SharePoint, SQL and others.** Many of the technologies it connects with do not easily have text based interfaces, and might not even become directly available from more formal strict languages such as Python or Perl.

- **Helps everyone working in the field of Microsoft.** Systems administrators are not only the ones who can greatly benefit from the functions and benefits of Powershell. The software supports end-users with no interruption and create a GUI interface for the support staff. This interface can easily be altered by non-developers.

- **A great invention in the Microsoft.** We can expect that Powershell will not go away that easily, as many have seen its major influence especially in the Microsoft Common Engineering Criteria. In most cases, Powershell is being used by Microsoft to develop the GUI management for its underlying products. Microsoft is always in support of the Powershell for hosted and on-premise solutions.

Now that you've learned the basic information about Powershell and its many different benefits, let us now take an overview on how this software works with Microsoft.

When it comes to rich command tools and line interfaces, Microsoft has been a bit behind this area. Powershell was considered as Microsoft's ideal solution to those developers who require such abilities. Huge thanks to the software's .NET Framework base, as it offers some excellent scripting abilities.

Let's give an example of how Powershell works with Microsoft, let's say Powershell for Microsoft Exchange Server.

Contrary to what some people believe, learning Powershell is not a difficult activity. As a matter of fact, you will have the opportunity to begin using this programming software instantly if you are running some commands in a CMD prompt. On the other hand, Exchange Server administrators have an edge among other IT professionals since the Exchange Management Consoles (EMC) states the equivalent Powershell directs to carry out similar tasks within the shell that you just done in the console. Not only that! Along with Office 365, Exchange Server offers ample amount of opportunities to utilize Powershell on a regular basis.

So, how would you get started with Powershell for Microsoft Exchange Server?

An excellent way to begin with Powershell is by taking your regular routine tasks and doing them in the shell. This venture will be made easier than making use of the management console. How to do this? Simply take notes as you carry out a GUI administration activity, copy the commands of Powershell that the Exchange Server will show you, and then use the shell when you perform similar task in the future.

Microsoft open source Powershell and create a version available for Mac OS X and Linux.

Microsoft has recently made the releases of

Powershell Core available on Mac OS X and Linux (Ubuntu, CentOS and Red Hat). More platforms are expected to be released in the coming years. Powershell is .NET based, thus Microsoft required .NET on another platforms to bring Powershell to any other platforms. Those who want to regulate on a particular set of tools will definitely want this, as well as those who manage diverse estates.

WHEN AND HOW POWERSHELL CAN BE USED

What can you do with Powershell? Microsoft professionally designed this software program to help users automate and solve lots of complex administration tasks in a quick manner. For instance, Powershell can be used to show each USB device installed on one or more computers within a network. You can otherwise set a lengthy task to be operated in the background while doing other essential work. What's more, this software is also an ideal option for killing courses of action that are very slow in responding or filter particular information on computers and send it in the format of HTML.

Other cool, efficient things you can do with Powershell include:

- *Performing your most preferred CMD tasks*

Users can definitely stop with the use of CMD and begin carrying out all of those similar tasks in Powershell. This eventually makes the learning a bit simpler and quicker while helping you become more accustomed to the interface. Though a 3-letter launcher such as cmd is not accessible from the run prompt, the software will do the task on your behalf. Also, you can be able to dole out a shortcut key to the software so that Ctrl + Shift + P will launch it in a direct manner.

- *Using PSDrive for viewing beyond just drives*

The PSDrive command allows every user to see the items of the Windows background more than just traditional network, removable or local drives. You are required to enter a command before getting into the registry. Afterward, you'll be transported in the hive of registry and view or even delete items you want.

- *Setting a time-consuming task*

Have a cmdlet that consumes much of your time? Powershell is the best alternative to sending the cmdlet to the background for completion. This way, users are given the chance to send a set if commands to implement right away - all while allowing you to complete on your own schedule. By following a command, you can easily query Powershell about the status of the tasks available.

- ***Working from the keyboard***

If you're familiar with the environment of Microsoft SQL Query Analyzer, you will surely appreciate some of the keyboard shortcuts it offers. When you use Graphic Powershell, you can opt for a single or even several lines and utilize them through pressing the F5 key. This will help you save time in testing and editing.

- ***Export NTFS file permissions, be that recursive or not***

We all know that handling NTFS permissions is not a simple task, as it is an entire separate thing. When you use Powershell, you can easily export these permissions to audit access. You can even view ACLs or access control lists for security configuration. This is highly beneficial if you are running a scripted format cyclically. You can also use it on demand to identify a specific issue.

- **Other important use of Powershell:**

  o *Task automation*

  Solution providers find that implementing Powershell for task automation makes any job easier, such as merging old servers and developing virtual machines. It is no secret that IT staffs today spend plenty of time on repetitive jobs in order to complete varying tasks. Powershell offers a powerful language that anyone can use to write and implement scripts. These scripts can potentially remove cyclical tasks while adding important logic to accomplish complicated jobs. VMN is completely built on above Powershell, therefore, no matter which an administrator does in the Administration Console can be achieved through Powershell cmdlets as well. If an administrator is able to convert numerous manual work in Powershell scripts, it will be quite simpler for him to perform some heavy works or lifting.

  Some Powershell scripts control the VMM cmdlets to complete activities in VM, which makes it a lot easier for administrators to implement repetitive actions and get fast status on the physical condition of VMM objects.

o *Designing virtual machines*

In VMM, users will be given various ways on how to develop and design a virtual machine. Start by getting a connection to the VMM server and creating the job group ID. Get the final command and enter your VM name. You are now ready to make a virtual NIC and a virtual DVD. Delete if your HW profile has similar name. Make a new hardware profile through the user interface and make a new VHD for the VM. Get the hosts as well as their ratings for the HW profile of VM. Order the ratings of the host and identify if you have at least one positive star rating for the VM. If you got multiple results, it is best to choose the top one.

o *Physical to Virtual Conversion*

VMM makes merging old servers a waft using a simple wizard to modify physical servers, also called P2V or Physical to Virtual Conversion. Users will begin by getting connection to the VMM server and getting the administrative recommendations to have an access to the source machine. Get the host needed for this VM or virtual machine and set off the asynchronous physical to virtual conversion.

○ *Running scripts on isolated or remote computers*

In handling computers using Powershell, users are crucially given three options: Enter-PPSession cmdlet, Invoke-Command cmdlet and cmdlets that provide a ComputerName parameter. However, many considered that the best way to control Powershell remoting is through invoke-command cmdlet. This cmdlet enables you to use Powershell commands on many different remote computers that include cmdlet that do not mark the -ComputerName parameter. There are 2 ways to connect to remote computers through invoke-command. You can either make use of -ComputerName parameter for handling Windows machine or pass the – ConnectionUri parameter for managing backend applications.

o *Making active directory accounts*

In the world of enterprise, provisioning user accounts in Active Directory is an essential part of the job of administrators on a regular basis. Newly employed staff need to have their own user accounts before logging onto the domain-joined laptop computers or desktop assigned to them. Powershell is an excellent way to create new accounts for controlling the clout of scripting to mechanize repetitive tasks.

o *Managing Accounts*

Not a big problem if you are not a computer wizard, because Powershell makes the process simpler for you to create and manage a user account. It offers considerable flexibility in how the procedure can be performed in Windows Server 2012 R2 and Windows Server 2012. As soon as you key in "Get-Command" *ADUser, you will be presented with 4 cmdlets to manage user accounts:

  ▪ Get-ADUser – allows you to get one or multiple Active

Directory users so you can conduct some activities with them.

- New-ADUser – allows you to craft a new Active Directory user.

- Remove-ADUser – takes the specific user out from Active Directory.

- Set-ADUser – changes the specific user from Active Directory.

o *Managing files and folders*

There are plenty of softwares available in the market, designed to manage different files and folders. The only downfall is that, they can be restricting. This is where Powershell enters the picture.

In spite of the niche you are involved in, chances are a few parts of your everyday routine includes managing folders and files in some way - whether it is looking for massive files or moving folders to a server or location. In situations where tedious repeated tasks that damper your producitivity on core tasks, automation can definitely become a life saver, of course with the use of Powershell.

o *Finding folders and files*

In the old years of computer, the DIR command is considered as one of the first popular tools that administrators learn. But for those who are new to the process, DIR would record the folders and files listed in the specified directory. The same command has been featured by Powershell. It is in the type of Get-ChildItem cmdlet. This form of command enables users to develop a file listing in a directory. You can work on the files either through assigning the end product to a variable or using a piped command. Get-ChildItem adds the capacity to restrict the result to a folder or file by using the -Directory or -File switches in Powershell. Use the -Force switch to find out system or hidden files.

o *Copying, deleting and moving files*

As anyone would expect, Powershell is able to complete standard file work on multiple objects in just one pass. Users can make use of Copy-Item cmdlet when copying one or numerous folders or files from a single location. If you want to move a file or folder, the Move-Item cmdlet is such a big advantage. Want to delete some items? Not a tedious task with Powershell. Simply use the Remove-Item cmdlet. The -Recurse will help you delete a folder or file and its contents. As easy as that!

o *Syncing files*

Basically, syncing is copying files in a smarter manner. It involves reading the whole contents or other contents of a file, analyzing the difference and finally, making a decision about the files you'll need to copy. Syncing can be done in a number of ways, but the best option is through Powershell. How?

- Identify each folder's location.
- Learn everything in each of the folders you have chosen.

- Compare them using Compare-Object cmdlet. This will enable you to determine two different collections. If all of the collections are similar, they will output nothing.
- Read each of the files in foreach loop and check out which sides that must be copied from and to.

o *Allowing event logging*

For those who are looking to extend the abilities of Powershell Remoting in the environment, you might want to try or allow Powershell Module logging for event logging of any Powershell command. You can carry this out and allow WinRM with HTTPs to secure the business. How to enable options for event logging? Simply download the Windows and server system, Windows 8.1 & Server 2012 ADMX files for instance.

Now, install the missing ADMX templates. Please note that this only requires you to install on a single machine throughout the environment - the one from which you're writing Group Policy. When running the installer, you should copy the file path once you set up the files. The installer doesn't import the files for you, but unloads them to a folder on the system.

The next process is finding the right ADMX file. It is important to ensure you are really getting the matching ADML file in the proper nested folder.

As soon as you find the ADML file, copy the matching file and the ADMX. This will be found in the right language folder. Overwrite the original files. If you're not able to do this, simply delete the originals and copy the new ones. If you fail to copy the ADML, chances are the GPMC will be peculiar.

o *Reading the event log*

When writing logging information, event logs serve as the common place for Windows - whether it is a warning, an error report or simply an informational log. You will be given numerous reasons as to why you should start opening Event Viewer and scrutinize the event logs. Some of them include: (1) checking for some errors after a sudden restart; (2) finding the previous time a user logged in the computer and determining its identity; and (3) checking why a particular service botched to start at a boot time.

Though Event Viewer has proven to be a useful tool, you must always be in search of a more efficient way to spend data sources such as the event logs. This is where we are going to take a glimpse at the Powershell's Get-WinEvent cmdlet. This cmdlet is known not just a flexible, but also a powerful way to pull data out of the event logs in scripts and interactive sessions.

Similar to other cmdlet of Powershell, Get-WinEvent offers incredible help that users need for their event log. With no parameters, this cmdlet brings back information on each single event in the event logs. In order to get to the specified events you need, you are required to pass one or several parameters for filtering the end product.

Some of the most typical parameters of Get-WinEvent include:

- -MaxEvents - constraints the number of events returned.
- -ProviderName - filters events made by the particular provider.
- -Oldest - arranges the events returned so the oldest ones will come first. By default, the most recent and newest events come first.
- -LogName - filters events in the specific log
- Writing to the event log

When something is not right, a good Powershell script is known to troubleshoot such issue in an easy manner. When making scripts, you should not only consider working as a mark of success, but that you've accounted for all potential paths that script might take once you encounter an error as well. Logging is one action that you can use in a script. Logging directly to your chosen event log is highly possible and simple using built-in Powershell cmdlets. New-Eventlog and Write-Eventlog are the cmdlets that you will be working with when writing to your event log.

These cmdlets of Powershell are ideal for writing messages to current event logs and creating new event logs. For instance, you will use the Write-EventLog cmdlet if you want to write to the Application event log. Before getting started, you'll first need to find out the parameters that this cmdlet requires. At a least amount, you will need Source, LogName (any event ID you want providing it is an integer), EntryType (event severity e.g. Warning, Error, FailureAudit, SuccessAudit or Information), Eventld and Message. These parameters are clear-cut.

o *Managing Events*

One of the various benefits of Powershell is that it can be used to simoly access any event log information and incorporate that information into the pipeline of Powershell. Users can easily integrate event commands into their scripts and write impromptu event commands. By using Powershell, you have access to event log information from remote

and local computers. But, bear in mind that
the process is not alike for the two. You
need to use the Get-EventLog cmdlet when
accessing local event information, while you
need to develop a
system.diagnostic.eventLog object when
accessing remote information.

○ *Automating repetitive Office 365 admin
 tasks*

If you are an Office 365 IT administrator
who is in search of the excellent tool to
automate recurring administrative tasks or
search for access added capabilities that
can't be found in Office 365 Admin Center.
Powershell aims to be a good solution.

But first, let's take a look at Office 365
admin center.

Office 365 admin center is popularly known
as out of the box solution that extents the
whole administration lifecycle - starting
from the set up to the support. It is properly
designed to handle the most frequent
administration tasks like editing and adding
users as well as setting service settings. But
in cases such as exporting user lists, groups
and other data, using numerous filters to

search through data and editing or adding a vast number of users, it is best to use Powershell to help you save a considerable amount of effort, time and other resources.

Powershell helps power users and IT professionals to automate and control the organization of the Windows operating applications and systems. One example is the Office 365. The cmdlets of Powershell enable users to perform tasks throughout the environment of Office 365 Powershell. These may include determining which mailboxes are not active, administering Office 365 certificate assignments and adding users to the Office 365 organization, among others.

o *Administering SharePoint*

The Powershell cmdlets you utilize in SharePoint will help you complete administrative tasks, no matter how simple or complex they may be.

Integrating SharePoint into Powershell brings in a lot of creative and interesting ways for any user to troubleshoot and gather important data. But similar to the case of other people, identifying where to start may find you quite puzzling. You're not alone! Good thing, there are various ways you can do to get started and benefit from what Powershell can offer for administering your SharePoint.

Before managing your SharePoint, it is initially advised to open not only the Powershell, but the Management Shell as well. This is because the commands you require won't be accessible. To help you get an idea of the things you can do, the Management Shell goes together with a number of commands to facilitate you.

- Get-Command-Module – gives list of the available commands to manage SharePoint. As we know, Powershell can be able to manage everything, thus you can see what you can do by restraining to the management module.
- Get-Member – see all the coming results. However, their differentiator is called the "Member Type". Here, you will see some results as "Property" and some as "Method".

How would you access Window Powershell for

SharePoint? Let's make SharePoint 2013 as an example.

You initially need to install SharePoint 2013. Appropriate Powershell cmdlets are nearly available in the SharePoint 2013 Management Shell. Most features of the SharePoint 2013 can be managed in the Management Shell. Users have the opportunity to design new site collections, user accounts, proxies, service applications, web applications, etc. The commands that you key in the Management Shell go back SharePoint objects derived from the Microsoft .NET Framework. You can either keep the objects within local variables for use later on or apply these items as input to successive commands.

Start the SharePoint Management Shell by clicking "Start" then the "Microsoft SharePoint 2013 Products. Afterward, click "SharePoint Management Shell". This is applicable if you are using Windows Server 2008 R2. But if you are making use of Windows Server 2012, click "SharePoint Management Shell" on the start screen. If the SharePoint Management Shell cannot be found on the start screen, right click "Computer", click "All Apps" and lastly, click "SharePoint Management Shell".

UNDERSTANDING POWERSHELL PIPELINE SCRIPTING AND HOSTING

Much has been said regarding how Powershell is new, different and exciting - although it is derived from the theory of command-line interface that have been around for years, basically in Linux and UNIX-based operating systems. However, the common term it shares with its past histories can make it quite easy to ignore the real uniqueness and flexibility of Windows Powershell, as well as its renowned suitability for the Windows environment.

Pipeline, scripting and hosting are the talked-about features of Powershell. Let us tackle each one of them.

Pipeline

The pipeline is considered a core in the concept of Window Powershell. Little seems sensible in Powershell with no perspective about pipeline. UNIX shells started the concept of pipeline, and then Cmd.exe imitated it. Powershell takes this concept to the next level.

The pipes' origin

As have mentioned earlier, UNIX shells originally launched the pipeline concept, and their work was popularly called the Thompson shell. It was highly archaic and featured only the most basic elements of scripting language without variables. The Thompson shell had a purposely modest design as its key goal was to implement programs. But, it was initiated as a main concept that enhanced on other shells - pipes. A user was able to redirect output and input to and from varying commands, such as redirecting command output to a specified file.

Later, this syntax was expanded to do and complete more complex tasks. Though the Thompson shell of Unix was extensively regarded as scarce by the moment UNIX version 6 was launched in 1975, the pipe concepts was well-rooted with shell users and developers and has been taken forward into some technologies available today.

What makes piping in Powershell so amazing? The fact is that anything in Powershell is an object - complete with methods and properties we can utilize. Even a text file is theoretically an assortment of string objects, with every line inside the file that acts as an independent and unique string object.

Fundamentals of pipeline

Simply think of the Powershell pipeline as the pipe's length. Commands set out in one end and objects surface the other. Though you are not able to see what is happening in the pipe, you can always give a few directions. In Powershell, the vertical bar (|) symbolizes the pipe. This indicates Powershell that you like to take the command's output and pipe or pass it as the input to the subsequent command. This type of concept has been around for some decades now in console-based shells, and is barely new to Window Powershell. The key difference is that, you're passing absolute objects rather than passing or piping text between commands.

If you are piping data from one command to another, there are cases when you must help the receiving command to be aware of the type of data it is accepting from the inputting pipe. This can be done thru forwarding the piped data to the specified parameter of the command. This idea is called pipeline parameter binding.

Being capable of piping objects from one cmdlet to next, or even from cmdlet to script, allows the creation of amazingly powerful one liners. These are known as simple strings of cmdlets connected to a long pipeline that additionally improve a pool of objects to exactly give users what they essentially need. Without any kind of programming or scripting, Powershell cmdlets roped together in a right pipeline to achieve notable, successful results.

Let me give you a simple pipeline example in Powershell.

The use of a pipeline expression is an excellent method to cultivate results until you attain what you exactly needs. If you are a beginner, it is recommended to break this down in numerous steps to avoid confusion. Below is an example.

First, you need to arrange every process in descending order. Do this using their Virtual Memory. If your Get-Process command provides you the expected result, you can now add the next pipeline step. If needed, you can continue adding steps to meet your target goal.

You'll also notice that you started with process objects, but Powershell gave you a measurement object by the last part of the pipelined expression. But if you are not able to get your desired result, return the command and then pipe the outputs to the Get-Member cmdlet in order to determine what is oozing from the pipeline.

Scripting

Powershell scripts provide a useful way for automating many different tasks. Maybe you are one of those who think of scripting as of enigmatic hieroglyphics, which can only be managed by the software experts. However, this is not entirely true as everyone is able to learn ways on how to run scripting and reap its productive results afterward. Scripting is developed logically, which IT adept individual or IT administrator can study and master.

Why scripting?

Various reasons are presented as to why scripting should not be overlooked. These include:

> I. *Minimizes the GUIs requirement* - one example is the Windows Server 2016 with and without GUI. Performance without GUI is much quicker than with; however, security is the most crucial argument. Windows.Server with no GUI requires much less restoring with. Thus, we can say that an OS with no GUI is more secure every time.
>
> II. *Minimizes human error* - users build automations, in which the values are filled or prefilled automatically or confirm the keyed in arguments before you fire up the next task.
>
> III. *Saves money and time* - scripting proves to be a money and time saver

once used. Through automating the tasks, supports desks are improved by one hundred percent efficiency. That's one of the great things about using scripting!

IV. *Builds standardization* - this stage depends on, if the user is doing it properly. Through standardization, you can be able to accomplish a higher quality work as well as reprocess your code for various use-cases.

V. *Important for new technologies* - since some tools these days don't have the capacity to handle various technologies.

VI. *Allows the development of new technologies* - as scripting boasts new cool features being integrated to ensure a smooth procedure from the beginning until the end. We can expect for new features in the coming years.

How scripting can be of great help? Here are some fundamental concepts that will help you as you begin building up Powershell scripts.

• PS1 files

A Powershell script is nothing beyond a simple text file. The file itself consists of a group of Powershell commands. Each command appears on a split line. Its filename should make use of the PS1. extension in order for the text file to be treated as a script of the Powershell.

• Running a script

Over the past years, users are required to navigate the path of the file and then enter the executable file's name so they can run this executable case from the command line. But, this old process doesn't work for Windows Powershell script. Basically, users will need to enter the complete path together with the filename in order to run a Powershell script. For instance, you could type C:\Scripts\Script.ps1 for executing a script with a name SCRIPT.PS1. Here, the exemption is that users can run a script by just entering the name if the folder holding the script is in the path of their system. A shortcut can also be used if you're already in the folder having the

script. Simply enter .\ and the name of
the script (e.g. .Script.ps1)

- **Variables**

Sometimes, pipelining alone doesn't get
the task done. In some cases, the output
is utilized immediately once you
pipeline the output of a command. You
may occasionally need to keep the
output a moment or two so you can use
or even reuse it shortly. This is where
variables enter the picture.

In Powershell, variables are responsible
for storing the full output of a command.
Let's say you want to put the list of
methods executing on a server as a
variable. For doing so, you might use $a
= Get-Process.

- **Breakpoints**

Unintended results can occur if you run
a newly developed Powershell script that
contains bugs. The best way to defend
yourself is by inserting breakpoints at
planned areas in your script. By doing
so, you are assured that the script works
as expected before processing the whole

thing.

Increase your productivity with Powershell scripting!

Hosting

As a human being, you can't really communicate with the engine of Powershell in a direct manner. Rather, a host application will allow you to do so. Integrated Script Environment (ISE) and PowerShell.exe are some examples of a host. These hosts 'spin up' a runspace, which is significantly an occurrence of the Powershell engine. As soon as you key in a command and click enter, the host builds a pipeline, jam the command into it and eventually, handles thr output.

Is it possible to create your own Powershell host?

Definitely, yes!

Once you run Powershell commands, it's actually the runspace that performs most of the execution work and handles the execution pipeline. Principally, the host is accountable for managing output and input streams to communicate with the runspace. In addition to Powershell ISE and PowerShell.exe, such examples of hosts are a custom console, WPF, Windows service applications or WinForms. The various hosts work together with the Powershell runspace after the scenes. When creating your own host, you also create a runspace instance and pass its commands to be executed.

How to host Window Powershell in the application

The Powershell class is highly important to achieve this process. This class offers procedures that make a pipeline of commands and execute these commands in a runspace. To help you create a host application, you are recommended to make use of the default runspace, which consists of the most important Powershell commands. On the other hand, you need to make a custom runspace if you want your application to show only a rift of the Powershell commands.

Using default runspace

If you choose to use the default runspace, you are now required to use the Powershell class methods for adding commands, scripts, parameters and statements.

- o Use the methods of the Window Powershell class to add pipeline commands.
- o Add parameters to the command through AddParameter method.
- o Simulate batching through the method of M:System.Management.Automation. Powershell.AddStatement. This adds an added statement to the pipeline's end.
- o Run a current script by labeling the AddScript method.

Building a custom runspace

Users can build a custom runspace that simply loads a particular split of all commands. You can do this to limit the capacity of a user to do operations or to improve performance.

- o Create an InitialSessionState object to load the entire integrated core Window Powershell. You could also call the M:System.Management.Automation.

Runspaces.InitialSessionState.Create
Default2 method to load the
commands in
Microsoft.Powershell.Core snapin.
o Create a constrain runspace. Do this
by creating a bare InitialSessionState
object through labeling the Create
method. Then, you can now add
commands to the InitialSessionState.

**Many ask: "How to host the Powershell
runtime?"**

If you're up in the market to answer this
question, well I must say you're in the right
place. To host the Powershell runtime in the
application, users need a few way for their
application to pass document in and out of
the Window Powershell environment and
state its fundamental commands to run. You
will need many classes from the developer's
insights, and these are defined in the
System.Management.Automation meeting
and 2 classes you should know about are
PSHost and PSHostUserInterface. When
you subclass these two interfaces, you can
easily communicate with Powershell from
your application judgment.

**How about adding a Powershell host to
vRealize Orchestrator (vRO)?**

The process is just made easier! Once you add a Powershell host to vRO, you have the opportunity to kick off Powershell scripts from the vSphere WebClient or from the vRO workflows. This ultimately makes your regular work a lot easier and hassle-free. Before adding a Powershell host to vRO, you will need Windows 2008 R2+ with Powershell 2.0+ and vRO Powershell Plug in v1.0.6.2442318, besides the vRealize Orchestrator itself.

POWERSHELL COMMANDS

Whether you need a fast refresher or simply getting started with Powershell, knowing the Powershell commands and their uses are highly crucial. Below, we have listed some of the most common Powershell commands, with fine points on when you should use them.

The foundation of Powershell commands are cmdlets. The experts at Microsoft developed numerous design strategies when creating Powershell cmdlets. First, the ability to simply deduce or discover cmdlet names. Also called cmdlets, Powershell commands are developed to be user-friendly with standardized syntax, which makes them easy to make powerful scripts or to utilize interactively from the line of commands.

Powershell commands or cmdlets make use of the non-verbal set-up such as Import-Csv, Stop-Service and Get-Service. The verb section tells the action to be carried out on the noun. Commands used to change something will typically start with the verb set. If you want to add a new unit to something, commands should often start with New or Add. In most cases, these combinations of verb-noun can be forecasted or guessed due to the standard naming convention.

So, let us take a look at the common Powershell commands for accomplishing tasks with Windows Powershell. These basic commands must get you started on the route to becoming a master.

    a.   **Get-Help** - the first cmdlet that all administrators need to learn. This command can be used if you want to get help with other command. For instance, type Get-Help -Name Get-Process if you need to determine how the Get-Process command works. Then, Windows will present thr entire command syntax. Also, the Get-Help command can be used with individual verbs and nouns.

    b.   **Get-ExecutionPolicy** - this is useful if you are working on a server that is unfamiliar to you. You should know the type of execution policy being utilized before trying to run a script. The Get-ExecutionPolicy command will be of utmost help.

c. **Get-Service -** gives a comprehensive list of every service installed on the systems. If you want a particular service, simply add the -Name switch and the service name. Windows will then display the state of the service.

d. **Get-Process -** if the Get-Service command is responsible for showing a list of available system services, the Get-Process command is accountable for displaying a list of every process that currently runs on the system.

e. **Set-ExecutionPolicy -** while users can make and accomplish Powershell scripts, Microsoft has hindered scripting by default to prevent malevolent codes from implementing in a Powershell environment. Instead, the Set-ExecutionPolicy command is recommended to use in order to control state of security around Powershell scripts. There are 4 levels of security:

(1) Restricted - the default execution policy and bolts Powershell down so they can be entered

interactively. In this level of security, Powershell scripts are disabled to run.

(2) Unrestricted - eliminates all the restrictions from the execution policy.

(3) Remote Signed - allows all locally developed Powershell scripts to run. However, scripts that are created remotely will only be allowed to run if they're signed by a reliable publisher.

(4) All Signed - scripts are allowed to run, only if they're also signed by a reliable publisher.

How to set an execution policy? Simply enter Set-ExecutionPolicy command after the policy name.

    f.   **Stop-Process -** important when a specified process has stopped working. As soon as you experience this situation, you are advised to utilize the Get-Process command in order to get the process ID or name for the process that has freeze up. Then, end the process through Stop-Process command. You can end the process based on its process ID or name. However, bear in mind that the process ID can change from one session to another.

    g.   **Get-EventLog -** Powershell can be used to

parse the event logs of your computer. Various parameters are available to help you regarding this matter, but you can practice the Get-EventLog command by just giving the -Log switch after the log file's name. For example, use Get-EventLog -Log "Application" when viewing the Application log.

h. **Export-CSV** - just as users can make an HTML file based on Powershell information, they can also export data from Powershell in CSV file they can open through Microsoft Excel. At a minimum, you need to give an output filename. For instance, you should use the command Get-Service | Export-CSV c:\service.csv when exporting the system services list to a CSV file.

i. **Set-ScheduledJob** - a new Powershell command and one of those functions that any system administrator should know how to carry out. Initiated in Powershell 3.0, this cmdlet offers a tool for operating almost any Powershell script on an intended schedule or at a particular time. What was not very easy in Powershell 3.0 was the capacity to run a designed job immediately. This makes Powershell 4.0 comes to the rescue as it added the keyword parameter RunNow for a much easier task.

j. **Get-Netnat** - part of the NetNat unit that contains commands such as Set-NetNat and New-NetNat. This ability to construct Network Address Translation (NAT) on remote systems is at the core of the hybrid cloud strategy of Microsoft, in which users can easily connect their on-premises systems to systems in the cloud, as well as interact as if they are on similar LAN. Get-NetNat makes the deletion and creation of virtual NAT connections through the running of a script.

k. **ConvertTo-HTML** - helps you create a document you can send to a person. In order to use this command, just duct the output from a specific command in the ConvertTo-HTML command. You'll be required to utilize the -Property switch so you can control which among the output properties presented will be integrated in the HTML. Later, you will provide a filename.

There are other Powershell commands available, and each of them plays an integral role to make the tasks easier and quicker to accomplish. It is necessary and important to learn and master each command so you'll not find it difficult to use one when needed for executing a particular task.

Files and Folders

In the previous page, you've learned that Window Powershell is one of the best software tools available for managing files and folders. Now, let us tackle this topic in a broad manner. This section provides information about carrying out file and folder management tasks with the use of Powershell. Since we've already tackled how to copy, move, delete, sync and find files and folders, the tasks we will include here are ways on how to zip items, unblock files from folders and sub-folders, rename multiple files, audit files and folders and change ownership of folder or file - all with the help of Powershell.

But first things first, how would you work with files and folders using Powershell? Well, cmdlets are the solution!

Windows Powershell actually offers 4 different methods to work with files and folders: DOS commands, Microsoft.NET Framework methods, Windows Management Instrumentation and cmdlets.

Though DOS commands, Microsoft.NET Framework methods and WMI can be of great help, many prefer using cmdlets to manage their files and folders. And, there are many cmdlets geared towards particular requirements. With the use of cmdlets, a person can be able to manage files and even file paths, besides working with the file contents.

Having said that let me give you some of the commonly used cmdlets that enable you to easily manage your files and folders.

Get-Item cmdlet

This cmdlet recovers the specific items from the specific locations. You can use the Get-Item cmdlet for navigating through various forms of data stores. Since it doesn't feature a default location, you need to provide at least one location through -Path parameter. The wildcard character (*) is used to retrieve any file content. The cmdlet returns the System.IO.DirectoryInfo objects, which consists of several methods and properties you can use.

Get-ChildItem cmdlet

The Get-ChildItem cmdlet is able to retrieve items contained within one or multiple specified locations. A location may be a file system box, like directory or even a location shown by a provider (e.g. certificate store or registry sub tree). In order to get the items in any subfolder, you may necessitate using -Recurse parameter. In addition to -Recurse parameter, this cmdlet also uses the -Force parameter (adds unseen files and system files to the output) and -Include parameter (retrieve particular items).

New-Item cmdlet

When it comes to performing the dual role of file and directory creator, the New-Item cmdlet doesn't frustrate its users. Not only that! It can also make registry entries and registry keys. When creating a file, you must include the -ItemType parameter and -Path parameter. During the process, you may experience getting an error. This only happens if your file with similar pathname exists by now. You may include -Force parameter so New-Item cmdlet will overwrite the current file.

Copy-Item cmdlet

The Copy-Item is considered as the Powershell's execution of the UNIX cp command and the DOS copy command, excluding that it is intended to work with the data given by a particular provider. The first 2 parameters of Copy-Item are -Destination and -Path. The -Destination parameter is used to indicate the exact location you want to copy an item, while the -Path parameter is used to indicate the item you like to copy. Because they are positional, their names can be gone astray.

Move-Item cmdlet

The Move-Item cmdlet can be compared to the Copy-Item cmdlet. As a matter of fact, the commands will act in much similar manner if you change Copy-Item with Move-Item. Excluding only that the original documents will be removed within the source folder. The only noteworthy difference is that, Powershell overwrites the current file in the location folder with no warning when you run similar Copy-Item command two times, while Move-Item is more careful in this matter. This cmdlet gives an error instead.

Rename-Item cmdlet

If you need to rename a source in a provider namespace of Powershell, the Rename-Item cmdlet proves to be very accessible. The first parameter of this cmdlet is -Path, while -NewName parameter follows. Rename-Item throws an error as soon as it identifies a path. -NewName and -Path are propositional parameters, thus users can skip the parameter names, providing of course that they are in the presumed positions.

Now that you have an idea about the different cmdlets you can use to work with files and folders using Powershell, let's proceed to the other ways in which Powershell can be of great importance when it comes to managing your files and folders.

Zipping files and folders

For the past years, we've been zipping items through different processes in Powershell. This range from 7zip libraries to Powershell Community Extensions or System.IO.Compression.FileSystem. There's actually nothing wrong with using any of these processes, but Powershell has recently launched various cmdlets to make the task less hassle on your part.

In zipping items, most people use the new cmdlet - Compress-Archive. It is part of the Microsoft.Powershell.Archive module. The exquisiteness of this cmdlet is that, users can be able to run through the whole directory and easily pipe the output in Compress-Archive and indicate the destination zip archive. But if you don't like to do this, simply have an assortment of items to be stored in the -Path parameter. There's one important thing you need to keep in mind when using Compress-Archive: you can't compress a file above 2GB in size since it makes use of the

System.IO.Compression.ZipArchive class to
compress the items.

Unblocking items from folders and sub-folders

You've downloaded an application component
online. This component contains msis, dlls, exes,
etc. But as soon as you right click on the
msis/dlls/cab files and choose the properties below
the general tab, you receive a message saying this
filename is blocked to protect the computer.

So, what's the best solution? Definitely not getting
alarmed or worried. Instead, take advantage of
Powershell command so you can unblock all the
items contained within the folders and subfolders in
just one go. This method is highly recommended
especially for beginners, as when it's executed
successfully, the issue will not happen even if you
copy the files to any other location. Simply run Get-
ChildItem <path to your folder> -Recurse |
Unblock-File for unblocking your files recursively.

Renaming multiple files

When it comes to renaming items within a
command-line environment, Powershell provides
more flexibility. Rename-Item and Dir are two
imperative commands you will need to accomplish
this task. Simply pipe the output of Dir to Rename-

Item and voila! As the name itself denotes, Rename-Item is used to rename items, while Dir lists the files in the existing directory.

Let's say you want to rename an item from "wordfile.docx" to "My Word File.docx". You can use the cmdlet rename-item "wordfile.docx" "My Word File.docx".

As you could expect, Powershell provides us with wonderful power to name our files. The Rename-Item cmdlet also offers features such as a -force switch (forces file renaming that are unavailable or locked), -recurse switch (apply the cmdlet to files inside a folder nested in that folder and -what if switch (describes possible things that could happen if the cmdlet was executed.

File and folder auditing

Often, particularly in enterprise environments, it is practical to keep track of activities - such as when files have been changes, what time and who changed them. This serves as the basis for file auditing. In this section, we aim to give you an idea on the fundamentals of getting folders and files auditing set up using Powershell.

File auditing is highly essential in business environments as it shows auditors a great path of the name of a person who has accessed a particular file and the exact time. If someone comes and requests you for a file recovery, just look at the audit logs and reports. This will allow you to identify when the data was removed. Then, use your chosen backup and recovery tool to revisit the previous date to when the item deletion happened and get it.

Changing ownership of a file or folder

While Explorer is proven useful for finding a file or folder and taking the ownership, you might consider using Powershell to do the same thing without missing out on a file or folder. Other than that, Powershell is said to be quick and easy to use when accomplishing this form of task.

Set-ACL can be used to do the entire process. All you need to do is get the ACL object of a folder to a different place in the home directory of the user. Make sure it had good permissions. You can now use it to the profile folder. Though there are unpredicted issues you may encounter, this process assures to generate expected result without consuming much of your time and effort.

There you have it, the excellent use of Powershell in managing files and folders. These are just some, because you can still find other ways where Powershell can be used for your file system. It is important to familiarize yourself with the different Powershell cmdlets so further errors or issues can be prevented.

SCRIPT CREATION BASICS

As have mentioned earlier, scripting is one of the most essential components of Window Powershell, and should be taken meticulous considerations before executing.

This page covers some essential facts on creating and running Powershell scripts. This document is designed as a concise guide for those who would like to leverage Powershell scripting in a more effective manner.

- **Creating Powershell script**

While there are many excellent scripting languages available, many still prefer spending time with Powershell. If you are using the newest version of Microsoft Windows, you've possibly got a version of it mounted.

So, how do you create a Powershell script?

Powershell saves scripts in the format of .ps1. Such example is C:\Scripts\My First Script.ps1, which was created both a folder and a file. You can use your own custom filenames and folder. Now, you can edit your own file and add some line. Afterwards, save the file and go back to the Powershell window. The commonly used method for running the scropt is by calling it & "C:\Scripts\My First Script.ps1". You can try that command.

Along the process, you may get an error saying that the scripts have been rendered inoperative on your system. Don't get easily alarmed when this situation happens, as this is a normal case. Powershell had enforced an execution policy in order to prevent the malicious scripts from operating on your system. These are Restricted, Unrestricted, RemoteSigned and AllSigned.

For your newly-created script to be utilized, you will need to change your execution policy to enable your script running. If you have not digitally signed your new script, the Unrestricted and RemoteSigned are the only options left to set the execution policy. You need to modify it to RemoteSigned.

For modifying the exchange policy, regenerate Powershell as an Administrator and run the command below:

- **Set-ExecutionPolicy RemoteSigned**

This command will then ask to confirm that you really like to modify the exchange policy. To verify, click "Y" for yes and then close and reopen the Powershell Window. After you restart it, try running the script again. So, finally! You are now able to create your first Powershell script.

- **Running Powershell script**

Powershell has a "secure by default" viewpoint, preventing any script from running. Thus, double clicking a script from the Windows Explorer would not execute it. Additionally, Powershell doesn't run scripts from the existing directory.

But, there's good news! Running Powershell scripts doesn't mean you need to be a Powershell guru. By simply following the steps given, you can successfully run it on your system.

How to get started?

- *Install Powershell*

If you are making use of Windows Vista or prior, you should download and install Powershell. Windows Server 2003 and Windows XP also need the Microsoft.NET.Framework 2.0. But if you are using Windows 7 or prior, there is no need for you to install Powershell as it comes preinstalled through the OS.

- *Set the execution policy of Powershell*

As I have mentioned above, Powershell is secure by default. The initial allusion of this philosophy is that Powershell would not allow scripts to run until the user explicitly provides consent to do so.

Enter Get-ExecutionPolicy in order to display the existing execution policy. To set the execution policy, the permissions of an administrator is highly required. In Vista and later, you need to run Powershell with eminent permissions if you are an administrator and UAC or User Account Control is enabled.

In order to execute Powershell under eminent permissions, right click the Powershell shortcut and select Run as administrator. But if you are logged on to Windows 2003 or XP, right click the shortcut and select Run as. Then, enter administrator account credentials.

 Many recommend setting the execution policy to RemoteSigned since it allows users to create and run scripts on their system without requiring them to sign using a code signing certificate. You can also make use of .adm file or administrative template that Microsoft offers. This template is important to allow you manage the execution policy of Powershell with a Group Policy Object.

- *Run the Powershell scripts*

Now that you've already configured the execution policy, it's best time to run Powershell scripts. To get started, open a Powershell window, key in the name of the script (with/without the .ps1 extension) after the script's parameters and then click Enter.

You can also cd the dir and begin the script with "./". The "./" represents the new directory. Powershell necessitates you to have that so you can prevent things found in the current directory from running mistakenly. For separating paths, use the slash (/) or backslash (\).

When running Powershell scripts, there are

important things you should take into account, initially about a new option in Powershell 2.0.

Once you right click a .ps1 file, you will see a Run with Powershell displayed on your computer screen. However, some advise not to use it because when you opt for this option, the window closes straight away after the script completes. Instead, run the scripts from a Powershell command. This is, by far, the best choice you can make.

You should handle spaces in a different way thancin Cmd.exe. When the pathname of a script consists of spaces, border it using double quotes in order to execute it in Cmd.exe.

Powershell doesn't run scripts from the existing directory. It makes use of the Path instead. If you key in a script's name (without its location) and find out it is not in the Path, Powershell would not run it. This is another feature of the secure by default in Powershell. The scripts are not allowed to run in the current directory to prevent an attacker from putting a hoax script in the existing directory with similar name as a commonly utilized command.

To overtly run a Powershell script from the current directory, you are required to prefix the name of the script either with ./ or .\. This is to let Powershell know you want to run the script from the existing location.

Since Powershell doesn't run scripts from the current directory, you are advised to make your own directory, add this to your Path and keep your scripts inside this directory. Doing so means avoiding problems in the long run.

Running Powershell script ls just made easier! As you can see, the processes involved in running a Powershell script can be easily achieved even though you have little or no knowledge in scripting. By just following the above mentioned simple steps, running your scripts is just easy as 123!

CONCLUSION

Thinking that Powershell is only suited in larger areas? Well, you may be thinking the wrong way! No matter how small or big the environment you are working, or how simple or complicated the tasks you are dealing with in office, you may realize what Powershell can offer for your overall productivity as well as that of your business. Especially if you spend much of your time writing scripts, Powershell can be considered as your real friend.

Largely automating new user creation. Writing scripts that pulls documents from the merchant's site and dropping them in the accounting package. Collecting important IT documentation zipping it and sending to the business managers. These are just some of the intricate tasks that you can turn into simple ones when you choose Powershell as your fundamental software tool. Particularly for those who carry out repetitive tasks, gone are the days when you need to stick yourself on various tools that claim to make your activities hassle-free, where in fact can only make the job quite complicated.

From the day Powershell made a public appearance and captured the interest of thousands of individuals and businesses around the world, many have attempted to offer Powershell training or education. With so many options available, finding the right resource may be quite confusing. Choose a service provider or a company that boasts in-depth knowledge about Powershell. It should also provide you with the tools needed to help you understand and master the nuts and bolts of Window Powershell.

Powershell may seem complicated at first, but as soon as you learn and master its concept, featured and components, you can easily share the same learning to other people. All it takes is just enough amount of time and effort to finally acquaint yourself with its basic and complex concepts.

May this book serve as your guide throughout exploring the beauty and essentiality of Window Powershell. As we are living in the modern age, we can expect for a more innovative ways on how to maximize the use of Powershell to make our day to day activities a lot easier and more convenient.

-- David Chang

www.ingramcontent.com/pod-product-compliance
Lightning Source LLC
Chambersburg PA
CBHW061031050326
40689CB00012B/2768